A SIMPLE GUIDE

TO

HOTEL

HOUSEKEEPING MANAGEMENT

Lynton Viñas (Frye)

This book is written in Canadian English

A SIMPLE GUIDE TO HOTEL HOUSEKEEPING MANAGEMENT

TO:
Jasmin Tshangana

Catalogue Number: 2020-2453689

An Educational Research Associates Publication
ISBN: 978-1-928183-47-1
Distributed by

Fireside Books – Victoria, British Columbia
Part of the Peninsula Publishing Consortium

Lynton Viñas (Frye)

A SIMPLE GUIDE TO HOTEL HOUSEKEEPING MANAGEMENT

TABLE OF CONTENTS

Prologue...........5
Memories That Will Last a Lifetime
Chapter 1..........9
Duties of Housekeeping Department
Chapter 2.........17
Useful Terminology
Chapter 3..........22
Organization of the Housekeeping Department
Chapter 4.........41
Types of Hotels
Chapter 5.........55
Standard Procedures for Cleaning
Chapter 6..........81
Room Area Procedures
Chapter 7..........99
Procedural Issues
Chapter 8.........111

A SIMPLE GUIDE TO HOTEL HOUSEKEEPING MANAGEMENT

ABOUT THE AUTHOR

Lynton Viñas has been a manager and marketing guru for spas, private schools and beauty facilities, having worked her way up through the ranks. She is an accomplished singer and dancer who has performed at a variety of venues throughout Asia and Africa, and studied at the Cambridge School of Law and at the renowned International Hotel School in Cape Town, South Africa. She is from Cavite, Philippines and lives on Vancouver Island, British Columbia, Canada.

She has worked at the five stars Mandela-Rhodes Hotel Suites, the African Pride and the Fire and Ice Protea Hotels in Cape Town, South Africa and was a trouble-shooting manager for the Index Spa chain in the Philippines. She is the author of many articles on management in the spa and hotel industries, as well as the following books: *Haunted Hotels: Transitory Dances with the Dead, Grand Hotels: Reflections on Timeless Architectural Treasures, Astonishingly Remarkable and Unusual Hotels* and *A Concise Guide for Operating a Restaurant.*

Lynton Viñas (Frye)

A SIMPLE GUIDE TO HOTEL HOUSEKEEPING MANAGEMENT

Prologue

Memories That Will Last a Lifetime

"Don't stress. We will clean up the mess."

Housekeeping Department Moto by Lynton Viñas

Housekeeping is an operational department which is responsible for the cleanliness, the maintenance, the aesthetic upkeep of rooms and buildings, the public areas and the general surroundings that lead to a positive presentation of the place of business. The effort that the housekeeping department makes in making sure a place is spotlessly clean has a direct effect on the success of the business. Although it is an ancillary service, the housekeeping department contributes in a major way to the ultimate success of any place of business. No matter how excellent the service, no matter how luxurious the surroundings, if the place is not clean it has a negative effect.

Housekeeping is responsible for generating the first impression on a guest's mind. The housekeeping efforts clearly show how the hotel or other place of business will take care of its guests. Sparkling cleanliness is the precursor to what one can expect from a place of business.

I was once hired, while attending a hotel school, as a marketing manager for a struggling luxury hotel in Cape Town, South Africa, and when I asked the Board of Directors about the housekeeping department, they all stared in disbelief at me until one rather gruff individual said, "What does the housekeeping department have to do with marketing?"

A SIMPLE GUIDE TO HOTEL HOUSEKEEPING MANAGEMENT

My reply, "It is the most important part of marketing. It is the cherry on top of the whip cream when you order a chocolate Sunday."

I am sure they all thought they had made a big mistake in hiring me, but I must honestly say that it is easy for the people in suits, ties and/or tailored uniforms prancing about a luxurious lobby in an architecturally grand building to look at the housekeeping department as less than equal in the grand scheme of things. The truth is that this department is at the very heart of any marketing effort, because it is housekeeping's job to make sure the surroundings are spotlessly clean. Cleaners are the people who put the shine on the car, put the sparkle in the water and put the sizzle in the steak.

If you are a housekeeping manager, you are in a sometimes unappreciated position, but despite its complexities you will find it a rewarding career which lends great satisfaction, because you are not only delivering a service but you are also creating exceptional experiences for valuable guests, whether they are business travellers, people out for a weekend getaway, a newlywed couple on their honeymoon, a high school team travelling for a weekend hockey tournament or a group of conventioneers having a rousing good time. You are creating the impression that will solidify memories that will last a lifetime.

Chapter 1

Duties of Housekeeping Department

"Every job is a self-portrait. Autograph your work with excellence." ......Lynton Viñas Frye

<u>What is Housekeeping?</u>

Housekeeping means performing all the duties towards cleaning, maintaining orderliness and working as a team to guarantee that a place is as spotlessly clean as humanly possible. In the case of hotels, the housekeeping duties involve maintaining the hotel to the best possible state in terms of cleanliness; and thereby, creating a desirable ambience. The housekeeping department is responsible for more than just cleaning rooms. There must be an intense devotion to maintaining the equipment and safely utilizing proper chemicals in order to insure proper hygienic conditions. The laundry is often done in house or it can be sent out, but either way, the housekeeping department must assure it is done to the highest standards and there should never be any tears or flayed ends in linens or towels.

An often overlooked function for the department is pest control. Any sign of pests should be addressed immediately by arranging with the proper department for sanitizing and assuring proper measures are instituted to both clean and de-pest, in order to make sure any future infestation may be avoided. Cleaning a room is more than vacuuming, dusting and changing linens. It also includes attention to the furniture, fittings and fixtures of the entire hotel.

A SIMPLE GUIDE TO HOTEL HOUSEKEEPING MANAGEMENT

To understand the expanse or scope of housekeeping, it is imperative to understand the divisions of hotel.

Divisions of a Hotel

Administration

The General Manager, Assistant GM and ancillary staff in their offices.

Front Office

It is responsible for guest check-in and check-out, mail and information services and concierge services such as tour booking, reserving theatre seats and restaurant reservations and providing airport transportation service, etc.

Food and Beverage

Food and Beverage Departments are responsible for preparing menus, foods and managing the inventory of food and beverage items. It includes food and beverage preparation and service for the restaurants, lounges, coffee shops, bars, events and room service.

Uniformed Service Department

It includes parking and door attendants, drivers, porters and bell attendants. Of course, it also includes the concierge.

Housekeeping

Housekeeping includes the duties of keeping the areas of the hotel clean, tidy, hygienic and pleasant. It also includes the duties pertaining to decoration of the hotel premises.

Sales and Marketing

All sales, services, advertising, promotions and public relations are taken care of by this team.

Security

The security manager and security workers keep the property safe and secure from internal and external hazards. This department is sometimes contracted out.

Accounts

This department conducts all financial activities like producing bills and receiving payments, computing employees' compensations and delivering payments. They also carry out the activities such as compiling monthly and annual income statements, depositing and securing cash, and controlling and monitoring assets.

Maintenance

The Maintenance Department is responsible for the maintenance of the property. It takes care of repairing furniture and fixtures and painting the required areas. When the hotel is small, these works are contracted from an outside agency.

Engineering and Technology

This department is responsible for keeping all of the vital equipment operational. These duties include maintaining telephone, hotel management software, internet etc. It is also responsible for implementing any changes required such as upgrading the software and hardware.

Human Resource Department

The Human Resource Department is responsible for interviewing and recruiting qualified staff to be placed in appropriate positions. They also conduct exit interviews for the employees who wish to quit. It works to set wages and salaries based on regional market rates and ensures that the hotel meets safety and health administration standards.

In all these departments, the efforts of the housekeeping department are overt. They are directly visible to the guests even before they try food or avail themselves of other amenities. Housekeeping creates the first impression in the guests' minds. Hence, this department is the heart of the hotel business.

Housekeeping Department Structure in Hotel

The layout of the housekeeping department depends on the total number of guestrooms, outlets and required staff. The following areas of the department are the most prominent ones, but may not be present in all hotels:

Office of the Executive Housekeeper - The administrative work of the department is carried out here.

Housekeeping Control Desk - It is accessible 24 hours a day. The housekeeping staff reports at the start and end of the shift here. There are notice boards, storage shelves, registers, a lost and found cupboard and key-hanger matrix. If a time clock is utilized, it is usually located in this area.

Laundry Area - Washing, ironing, dry cleaning, folding of linen and staff uniform maintenance takes place here. (Sometimes this function is outsourced.)

Linen Room - Here, the linen such as bed-sheets, towels, pillow cases, etc. are stored, collected and carried to the required places.

Uniform Room - The staff uniforms are collected, stored and distributed from here.

Tailor Room - Here, stitching and repairing of linen and uniforms takes place.

Housekeeping Stores - It is a storage area where the cleaning equipment and items and guest supplies are securely stored.

Flower Room - It is an air-conditioned room with worktables, sink and water supply, cupboards to store vases and stones and a counter.

A SIMPLE GUIDE TO HOTEL HOUSEKEEPING MANAGEMENT

Lost and found - stores all the items left by the guests. It directly communicates with the front office desk, as that is wherre the guests tend to first enquire about their lost articles.

<u>Housekeeping – Areas of Responsibility</u>

The housekeeping department is responsible for keeping the following areas clean and tidy.

Guest Rooms

Guest Bathrooms

Public Areas such as Lobby and Lifts

Banquets and Conference Halls

Parking Area

Sales and Administration Offices

Garden/Pool Area

Outside Areas may also be designated as another responsibility, or it may be outsourced.

Apart from the cleaning task, the housekeeping department is responsible for handling keys for each floor. In addition, it manages the laundry, which is often, at some places, considered a sub-department of housekeeping.

Lynton Viñas (Frye)

Chapter 2

Useful Terminology

"There is opportunity in every difficulty."

.........Lynton Viñas Frye

Terms Used in Hotel Housekeeping

The following are commonly used terms in the housekeeping department, but this is, by no means, a complete list, as each hotel is unique and will have terms relative to each one individually.

1.   Contingency plan: Planning done for uncertain events.

A SIMPLE GUIDE TO HOTEL HOUSEKEEPING MANAGEMENT

2.   Lounge: A place in a hotel where a guest can sit back or relax. It is in public area furnished for relaxation.

3.   Damp-dusting: The method of cleaning where the items to be cleaned are wiped with a damp cloth.

4.   Bridge the bed: joining of two beds.

5.   Crinkle sheet: distinctive woven sheets to cover and protect the blanket.

6.   Nappery: table linen.

7.   Roll out: removal of extra bed from the rooms when the guest checks out.

8.   Jonny mop: toilet brush.

9.   Pallet: thin weight mattress.

10.   Amenity: a service or item offered to a guest at no extra cost.

11.   Back of the house: the functional area of hotels in which guests are not allowed to go.

12.   Back to back: describes a heavy rate check out and check-in on the same date which requires precise coordination.

13.	Turn down service: special service provided by the housekeeping department in which a room attendant enters the guest room in the evening to make the night bed and to replenish any items that are necessary.

14.	Hand-caddy: a portable container for storing and transporting cleaning supplies carried on a maid cart.

15.	Lobby Area: provided near the reception as a common meeting place for all the guests.

16.	Hopper: strong metal container for disposing of garbage.

17.	Sani-bin: metal bin with kept in a wash room for throwing disposed paper towels.

18.	Team cleaning: group of housekeeping staff working together in order to achieve the same goals.

19.	Wardrobe: tall cabinet or closet for keeping clothes.

20.	Candle-wick: soft cotton thread which makes the candle burn.

A SIMPLE GUIDE TO HOTEL HOUSEKEEPING MANAGEMENT

21.   Pilferage: the crime of taking someone's property without permission.

22.   Crease: line made on linen by folding or pressing.

23.   Frequency schedule: a schedule which indicates how often an area in a hotel has to be cleaned.

24.   Accommodation check list: list to help the housekeeping staff check all the items inside the room.

25.   Bath linen: includes bath towel, hand towel, face towel, shower step towel, etc.

26.   Cleaning supplies: cleaning agents and supplies for sanitizing a guest room.

27.   Water closet: sanitary fittings consisting of toilet bowl and cistern.

28.   Room status report: report that allows the housekeeping department to convey the present status of a room.

29.   Routine maintenance: activities related to general up-keep of a property.

Lynton Viñas (Frye)

30.   R.D.M. (Room division manager): a person who heads the department responsible for guest rooms, including front office and the housekeeping department.

Useful Abbreviations Used in Housekeeping

1.   G.R.A - Guest room attendant
2.   C/O - Check out
3.   C - Cleaned
4.   C/L - Check list
5.   O - Occupied
6.   V - Vacant
7.   O.O.O. - Out of order
8.   B.T. - Bath towel
9.   H.T. - Hand towel
10.   F.T. - Face towel
11.   D.N.D- Do not disturb
12.   D.L. - Double locked
13.   O.P.L. - ON/OFF premises laundry
14.   P.T.E. - Part time employee
15.   F.T.E. - Full time employee
16.   H.W.C. - Handle with care

17. W.C. - Water closet

18. S.B. - Scanty baggage

19. D.R. - Departure room

20. N.C and N.C - Not cleaned and not checked.

21. ASAP - As Soon As Possible

22. NY - Not Yet

23. CU - Check Up

24. FYI – For Your Information

Chapter 3

Organization of the Housekeeping Department

"No hotel can survive in the modern era of hospitality without a highly efficient housekeeping department that promotes the brand."...Lara Li

The housekeeping department carries out multiple tasks at three levels: managerial, supervisory and operational. There are probably no two housekeeping departments organized exactly the same way; however, the following chart reflects the norm for many hotels.

A SIMPLE GUIDE TO HOTEL HOUSEKEEPING MANAGEMENT

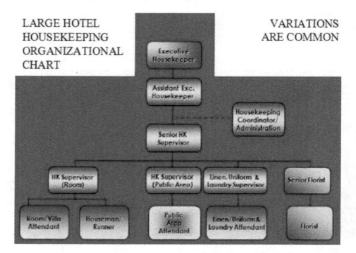

LARGE HOTEL HOUSEKEEPING ORGANIZATIONAL CHART

VARIATIONS ARE COMMON

Head and Deputy Head of Housekeeping

The jobs of the head and deputy head of housekeeping are generally shared, with the head delegating many, sometimes all, of the following:

1. Training the new hires and motivating the new employees.

2. Establishing Standard Operating Procedures (SOPs) for cleaning and decorating.

3. Monitoring regular inventory of guest supplies.

4. Monitoring housekeeping equipment and linen.

5. Evaluating employee performance, and handling their training, promotions and transfers.

6. Organizing flower arrangements for events.

7. Presenting the estimate of the required budget to the General Manager of the hotel.

Supervisors of Housekeeping

The supervisors report to the Assistant/Deputy Housekeeping Manager. Their positions and their respective responsibilities include:

1. Assigning Floor Supervisors

2. Issuing keys to the room attendants.

3. Coordinating floor operations and tray clearance with room attendants.

4. Inspecting rooms for readiness and reporting to the front office when done.

5. Catering for VIP facilities and providing special supplies such as drinking water and arranging baby-sitting provisions.

Public Area Supervisor

1. Checking all linen for needed repairs.

2. Ensuring that cleanliness is maintained at all times in public areas such as the lobby, lifts, parking, swimming pool, coffee shop, conference hall, banquet hall and restaurant.

3. Ensuring banquet and conference halls are well kept and ready for use.

4. Ensuring the concerned operating staff is available as per the schedule.

Night Supervisor

This person ensures the proper provision of guest supplies such as water, extra bedding, fans and towels, ensures the operating staff working at night follows all cleaning SOPs. Many medium or small hotels will assign this task to the night desk clerk.

Uniform Room Supervisor

Provides clean, ironed and fresh uniforms to the hotel staff. Suggests procurement of any uniforms required, checks repaired linen, keeps track of number and condition of uniforms.

Linen Room Supervisor

A SIMPLE GUIDE TO HOTEL HOUSEKEEPING MANAGEMENT

Inspects linen and sends it to laundry and for ironing. Maintains linen influx and out flux register. Checks repaired linen from tailor room and suggests replacement if required.

Operating Staff / Attendants

The positions and responsibilities of the Operating Staff/Attendants are explained below.

Uniform Room Attendant

(1) Collecting uniforms of staff at the end of every shift and maintaining them to be used for the next time. (2) Maintaining the shelves of uniforms and linens. (3) Giving out and taking back the uniforms from the staff.

Linen Room Attendant

(1) Segregating the dirty linen according to its type and sending it to the laundry. (2) Keeping track of linen count before and after laundry. (3) Stacking towels, bed sheets, pillowcases, table napkins separately into different sections of shelves.

Guest Room Attendant

A SIMPLE GUIDE TO HOTEL HOUSEKEEPING MANAGEMENT

(1) Cleaning guestrooms mid-stay and after departure. (2) Making beds. (3) Replacing dirty linens and towels. (4) Restocking guestroom amenities like toiletries, drinking glasses and notepads. (5) Removing garbage, recycling, and maintaining service trays. (6) Picking up and returning valet laundry items. (7) Replenishing hotel cleaners' trollies with supplies and linens for the next shift staff.

Storekeeper

(1) Reporting to the floor supervisor. (2) Keeping the count of cleaning equipment and items such as cleaners and detergents. (3) Generating requisitions to purchase the required material.

Public Area Attendants

(1) Keeping the parking, lobbies, guest rooms, lifts and corridors in immaculate condition. (2) Keeping these areas smelling fresh.

Night Shift Attendants

(1) Performing the night cleaning duties as identified.

Lynton Viñas (Frye)

A SIMPLE GUIDE TO HOTEL HOUSEKEEPING MANAGEMENT

(2) Reporting any hotel safety issues to the night supervisor.

There are certain professional qualities the housekeeping staff is required to possess. Although not all inclusive, the following are vital in order to project a positive image. (1) Personal hygiene and appearance must be meticulously maintained. This includes being well-groomed, having trimmed nails and hair and having a clean uniform so that a clean and pleasant appearance is always presented. A cooperative attitude is imperative, as is the ability to speak in an audible tone, so the guest can understand what is being said.

Interpersonal skills are an important part of the job, since there is often interaction with guests. Thus, the staff must display a positive attitude and have good listening skills to avoid any miscommunication. Remember that the guest expects integrity and dedicated service.

A SIMPLE GUIDE TO HOTEL HOUSEKEEPING MANAGEMENT

Hotel Housekeeping Principles

There are various principles followed by the housekeeping staff. They include cleaning and hygiene principles, safety and security principles, comfort and privacy principles, and finally, the décor detail.

Advantages of Good Housekeeping

Here are some prominent advantages the housekeeping department offers to its guests:

- Clean and hygienic atmosphere
- Comfortable and convenient stay
- Privacy
- Safety and security
- Provision of amenities
- Making guests have a positive experience

Purpose of Cleaning

Cleaning is conducted to remove harmful bacteria present in the dust deposited on the hotel property because of air pollution and to ameliorate the accumulation of germs from previous and current occupants. Remember that germs and bacteria can not only cause unhealthy effects on the guests but also the working staff. Cleanliness reduces the threat of any infections and offers a comfortable stay to the guests in the hotel.

Cleaning and Hygiene Principles

The worker must follow these given principles while cleaning.

• Carry out the cleaning procedures in sequence. For example, Sweeping - Dusting - Mopping/Suction Cleaning - Disinfecting - Air Freshening.

• Extreme care must be taken while cleaning, sanitizing and polishing, so as not to damage various surfaces and hamper their appearance.

• Cleaning should start from extreme inner end continuing towards exit.

• Always park the trolley such that it leaves space for corridor traffic.

• Take proper precautions while handling cleaning equipment, detergents and guest luggage.

- Always remove hard water stains and spider webs as soon as they occur.

- Never use guest room linen for cleaning or blocking the room entry.

Safety and Security Principles

The workers must follow the proscribed safety rules mentioned which may vary somewhat by the hotel.

- Protect the body from harmful chemicals by wearing thick gloves.

- Protect the eyes by wearing masks or goggles if required.

- Use a caution sign to mark wet floors.

- Clean spilled liquids immediately to reduce chances of slipping.

- Handle cleaning chemicals carefully while transporting, disposing or refilling the containers.

- Mix any chemicals required in the presence of proper ventilation.

- Do not open unlabeled chemical containers.

A SIMPLE GUIDE TO HOTEL HOUSEKEEPING MANAGEMENT

- Use swivel head mops to avoid inappropriate body posture while cleaning.

- Wear closed toe non-slip footwear while working.

- Use appropriate body postures while working to avoid cramps.

- Request for peer assistance while moving heavy loads such as furniture.

- Report to the supervisor in case of any accident due to mishandling of flammable or poisonous liquids.

- Keep the guests safe with the help of security department when necessary.

- Keep the guests' documents, ornaments or other articles safe.

Comfort and Privacy Principles

The housekeeping staff must follow the given principles with regard to comfort and privacy of the guest.

- Always remember comfort and privacy of the guests comes first.

- Clean the premises or rooms in the least destructive and disturbing manner.

- Enter the guest rooms by following appropriate procedure.

- Work towards the guests' satisfaction at all times.

Knowing and Handling Small Fire Hazards

It is vital for the housekeeping staff to have knowledge of the various types of fires and how to use fire extinguishers and immediate fire mediation measures. The staff must be trained to handle small fires, but to never put their lives at risk.

Fire is classified into the following types:

- Class A – Class A fire consists of ordinary combustibles such as wood, paper, trash or anything else that leaves ash behind. It needs water under high pressure to extinguish.

- Class B – This fire occurs in inflammable liquids such as oil and grease and requires blankets or sand to extinguish.

• Class C – This fire occurs in electrical equipment. Use of a non-conductive agent is required for extinguishing this type fire.

• Class K – Class K fires involve cooking oils, grease or animal fat and can be extinguished using Purple K, a typical agent found in kitchen or galley fire extinguishers.

Fire Extinguishers

Soda Acid extinguishers are used to put out class A fire. It sprays the compound with gaseous pressure. This is only good for small intensity fires. For large intensity and widely spread fires, water must be sprayed directly on the affected area with high pressure through the hoses. For putting out class B fires, Carbon Dioxide extinguishers are used. Carbon Dioxide fog extinguishers are used in case of small class C fires.

The housekeeping staff must place appropriate extinguishers near the fire prone areas and must know how to operate them under challenging conditions.

A SIMPLE GUIDE TO HOTEL HOUSEKEEPING MANAGEMENT

Importance of Decor in Housekeeping

The housekeeping staff is responsible for creating pleasant ambience in the hotel. This needs an aesthetic sense and an eye for detail. A guest is keen to visit the hotel if he or she finds a catchy ambience.

Housekeeping staff must intelligently use artificial waterfalls, large vases with neat and eye-catching flower arrangements, paintings, wall pieces, murals, lighting with appropriate luminance, candles, electric lamps or any rare antique pieces and take particular care to maintain them. This means the housekeeping staff should also be knowledgeable about various materials such as wood, organic and artificial fibres, stone, sand, glass, plastic and pigments to maintain an expensive hotel property, and not to use improper cleaning procedures which could have an adverse result on delicate items.

Hotel decors can be utiliized thematically depending on the local/international festivals and cultures. Décor is yet another important task that elevates guests' experience with the hotel.

The grander the hotel, the more detailed cleaning is required in order to elevate the ambiance to the maximum aesthetic level.

Rules for Housekeepers

The housekeepers represent the staff and create an image of the hotel by maintaining high standards, plus conducting themselves with professionalism while on the job. That is why an impeccable personal appearance is vital as it reflects the classiness of the hotel.

There are certain rules the housekeepers need to follow.

A SIMPLE GUIDE TO HOTEL HOUSEKEEPING MANAGEMENT

- Enter the floor with a meticulously clean and tidy uniform in a properly groomed manner. You are part of the hotel's image, a part of the décor.

- Only use the service lifts.

- Speak to the other working staff only when necessary.

- Do not walk by stamping the feet, run or jump on the hotel premises.

- Eat only in meal hours, not while cleaning.

- Stand completely outside the guest room while speaking to the guest to respect their privacy.

- Always keep the room doors open while cleaning.

- Greet the guests with a sincere smile and a "good morning, good afternoon, good evening" according to the time of the day. Let them know you appreciate their business.

- Never answer the guest room phone.

- Never use guest bathrooms.

Lynton Viñas (Frye)

A SIMPLE GUIDE TO HOTEL HOUSEKEEPING MANAGEMENT

- Familiarize themselves with the faces of guests. This is especially important for the security purposes, and greet them with a Mr. or Ms. So and So, as it lets them feel you are taking a personal interest in them and showing the proper respect.

- Never use a guest room for any unauthorized reason.

- Do not accept any gift from the guests and politely deny them. If the guest insists you take it and feels offended on denial, then mention the gift to the floor supervisor who can permit the attendant to take the gift out of the hotel.

Chapter 4

Types of Hotels

Hotels may not be home, but that is alright, because a hotel should actually be better than home. Do you get room service daily at home? Do you always get a cheerful greeting at home? At home do you have a concierge? Do you always have a spotlessly clean room and a dining area where you have a server who treats you like gold? A truly fine hotel, then, is the diamond that glistens with a sparkle that lights your soul.

A SIMPLE GUIDE TO HOTEL HOUSEKEEPING MANAGEMENT

Housekeeping is the primary task that provides superior service to its guests that makes them feel special. The hotel management and the executive of the housekeeping department must ensure that the housekeeping functions are performed well in the hotel irrespective of the target guest type, size of the hotel and its location.

The guest rooms are the primary source of a hotel's revenue; therefore, there are higher chances of retaining the guests if the rooms are pristinely clean and appealing.

Types of Hotels

The hotels can be categorized depending upon their size, location, target market and ownership.

Hotel Types by Size

Hotels are categorized by the number of rooms to which service is provided. For example –

- Up to 200 rooms – Small
- 200 to 399 rooms – Medium
- 400 to 700 rooms – Large
- More than 700 rooms – Mega

A SIMPLE GUIDE TO HOTEL HOUSEKEEPING MANAGEMENT

This category is useful if the management needs to compare different hotels within the same size. This has particular relevance in terms of the size of the housekeeping department.

Hotel Types by Location

• Airport Hotels − They are located near an airport, sometimes even in the airport. The guests in transit use them for short stays.

• Boatels − They are on houseboats.

• City Center − Located in the heart of the city near the commercial area.

• Motel − They are small hotels usually located on highways. Guests in transit use them.

• Suburban Hotels − They are located near urban areas.

• Floating Hotels − They are on the cruise ships, large lakes or rivers.

• Resorts − They are on the beaches, mountains, islands or on river banks.

• Rotels − They are hotels on wheels such as the Belmont Royal Scotsman or Antler's Inn.

- Self-Catering Hotels – They are located at the same premises where the owner stays.

Hotel Types by Target Market

These hotels are categorized depending upon the target market they serve. You will note some duplications from the previous list.

- Airport Hotels – They target the business clientele, airline passengers or any guests with cancelled or delayed flights.

- Business Hotels – They primarily cater to guests who are on business travel.

- Bed and Breakfast (B&B) – They are small hotels that target guests in transit or on a leisure tour. The owner of the B&B usually stays in the same premises and is responsible for serving breakfast to the guests.

- Casino Hotels – They target the guests interested in gambling.

- Resorts – They target high-income busy professionals who wish to spend time away from city, noise and crowds. They offer facilities such as a spa, tennis court, fitness centre, sailing, snorkelling and swimming.

• Self-Catering Hotels – They target long guests who prefer to cook for themselves. They offer a small kitchen and kitchen amenities with the guest room.

• Service Apartments – They are located in residential colonies. They provide long-term accommodation for guests. They need to execute an agreement with the guests for the stay of at least one month. All basic amenities such as kitchen, washing machine, dish washer and beds are provided with weekly housekeeping service as the norm.

• Suite Hotels – These hotels offer a living room and an en-suite bedroom. The professionals who need to interact with their clients/customers find these hotels a good choice because they can interact with their guests in small meetings without any interruption and sacrificing privacy.

Hotel Types by Ownership

A SIMPLE GUIDE TO HOTEL HOUSEKEEPING MANAGEMENT

B&B and self catering hotels are generally family owned hotels and do not operate under corporate policies and procedures.

A chain of hotels or group of hotels such as Taj, Ramada, Holiday Inn, etc. can have management affiliation with their other properties in the same group, or they may be franchised operations. Regardless, they are strictly governed by predetermined corporate policies.

Hotel Types by Star Rating

The star rating system is a guideline for a customer that denotes what to expect from the hotel service at the time of booking. However, there is no clear distinguishing method to divide hotels into various star rating categories today; but a guest can assume that more the number of stars, the more luxury provided by the hotel.

• One Star – A guest can expect a small hotel operated and managed by the owner and family. The ambience as more personal and the guest rooms have basic amenities. The restaurant

Lynton Viñas (Frye)

would be at a walking distance. There would be a small commercial area and a nearby public transportation hub.

• Two-Star – These hotels are mostly part of a chain of hotels that offer consistent quality but limited amenities. They are either small or medium size hotels with a phone and TV. They lack the convenience of room service, but provide a small on-site restaurant or one that is within easy walking distance of the premises.

• Three-Star – These hotels are usually located near a major business centre, express way, and/or shopping area. The rooms are clean and spacious and there are decorative lobbies. An on-site restaurant offers all meals such as breakfast, lunch and dinner. Valet and room service, fitness centre and a swimming pool are also available.

• Four-Star – This hotel would be large, often standing as a part of a cluster of similar hotels with a formal appearance and top notch services. The hotel would be located in the prime area of the city around shopping, dining and entertainment facilities. The guest can expect nicely furnished and clean rooms, restaurants, room service, valet parking and a fitness centre within the hotel premises.

• Five-Star – This hotel would be large and luxurious, offering the highest degree of room and personal service. It is generally beautiful architecture with elegance and style in mind. The guest rooms are equipped with high quality linens, large screen TV's, luxurious bathtubs and special outside views from the room. The hotel provides multiple eating places in its premises such as coffee shops, restaurants, poolside snack joint and bar. They also provide 24/7 room service, valet service and personal protection service.

Types of Hotel Rooms

The condition of hotel guest rooms maintained by the housekeeping department is the most vital and critical factor as far as customer satisfaction is concerned and there are different types of rooms.

A SIMPLE GUIDE TO HOTEL HOUSEKEEPING MANAGEMENT

1. Single Room − A room with the facility of a single bed. It is meant for single occupancy. It has an attached bathroom, a small dressing table, a small bedside table and generally a small writing table. Sometimes it has a single chair, too.

2. Double Room − A room with the facility of a double bed. There are variants in this type depending upon the size of the bed.

3. King Double Room (king size double bed)

4. Queen Double Room (with queen size double bed) It is equipped with adequate furniture such as dressing table and a writing table, a TV and a small fridge.

5. Deluxe Room − Any of the above with luxurious additions.

6. Single Deluxe and Double Deluxe variants. A deluxe room is well furnished. Some amenities are attached such as a bathroom, a dressing table, a bedside table, a small writing table, a TV and a small fridge. The floor is covered with carpet/wood and suitable for small families.

7. Double-Double (Twin Double) Room – This room provides two double beds with separate headboards. It is ideal for a family with two children below 12 years.

8. Twin Room – This room provides two single beds with separate headboards. It is meant for two independent people. It also has a single bedside table shared between the two beds.

9. Duplex Room – This type is composed of two rooms located on two different floors, connected with internal stairs.

10. Cabana – This type of room faces a body of water, a beach or a swimming pool. It generally has a large balcony.

11. Studio – They are twin adjacent rooms: A living room with sofa, coffee table and chairs and a bedroom. It is also equipped with a fan/air conditioner, a small kitchen corner and a dining area. The furniture is often compact.

12. Lanai – This room faces a landscape, a waterfall or a garden.

13. Suite – It is composed of one or more bedrooms, a living room and a dining area. It is excellent for the guests who prefer more space, wish to entertain their guests without interruption and without giving up privacy. There are various types of suites –

*Regular Suite – Best for business travelers.

*Penthouse Suite – More luxurious than the regular suite. It is provided with access to a terrace space right above the suite. It is aloof from the crowd and provides a bird's eye view of the city. It has all the amenities and structure similar to a regular suite.

*Presidential Suite – The best possible suite in the hotel.

14. Sico – This is a kind of multipurpose room, which can be used as a meeting room during the day and as a bedroom during the night. These rooms have special beds called Murphy Beds that can be folded entirely against a wall. This bed may or may not have headboard. The lower face of the

bed, which becomes visible after folding or placing upright, has a decorative wall paper, mirror, or a painting. After folding the bed, the room can accommodate seating for five to ten people.

VIP Amenities in the Hotel

VIP amenities are like the cherry on a sundae. The VIPs are treated with extra attention, pampered and afforded special care. Hotels provide the following amenities to the VIPs, depending upon their policies:

- Executive Front Desk or Executive Housekeeper escorting the guest up to the room.

- A welcome document kit containing a note from the General Manager (GM) of the hotel, a spa card, and a hotel map.

- Complete housekeeping service on call with daily linen change and cleaning.

- A snack kit often containing packed snacks, assorted nuts, fruits, cheese, or cookies and beverages.

A SIMPLE GUIDE TO HOTEL HOUSEKEEPING MANAGEMENT

- A vanity kit containing cotton balls, makeup removers, lip balm and au-de-cologne.

- A bathroom kit with soap dispenser, upgraded robe, tissue box, face mist, after-shower gel, cotton slippers, toilet mat and a terry mat.

- In special cases, a romance kit containing a bottle of wine or Champaign paired with chocolate dipped strawberries or bite size chocolates.

- Small bag packs for the kids below 12 years.

- A number of servings of award winning dessert.

Adding that extra touch to the room elevates the stay of guests from the commonplace to the extraordinary. For example, many of the very finest hotels have a turn-down service, where a housekeeper comes in and actually turns back the duvet and sheets for the guest. Many add an extra touch that was actually started back in 1937 by the famous actor, Cary Grant. Grant would take his most ardent paramours to some of the very finest hotels in the world, and before they would go to bed, while the lady was changing, he would turn back the covers and place a Lady Godiva chocolate on the pillow. Most hotels that have turn-down service still carry out this Lady Godiva tradition.

Chapter 5

Standard Procedures for Cleaning

Hotel Housekeeping Cleanings

Room cleaning is the major task the housekeeping force performs. It carries out cleanings before the guests are about to occupy their room, while they are staying in the hotel and immediately after the guests vacate the room. The housekeeping also cleans the public areas, which are often shared by a large number of guests at various times of the day.

A SIMPLE GUIDE TO HOTEL HOUSEKEEPING MANAGEMENT

Cleaning the Check-In Room

The check in rooms are cleaned when the guest is about to occupy the room. A checklist of room readiness is shared between the guest room supervisor and the guest room attendants. The supervisor inspects the readiness of the room for occupancy.

The guest room attendant performs the following cleanings:

• Checking power switches, air conditioner, TV and other electronic appliances for healthy condition.

• Making the bed with the fresh linen, pillow cases and bedside mat.

• Cleaning ashtrays, if there are smoking rooms, and dustbins - replacing if required; and putting fresh paper/tissues/cups in all dispensers.

• Checking stationery and vanity supplies. Replacing/refilling if required.

• Cleaning the bathroom floor, walls, toilet, shower area and tub.

A SIMPLE GUIDE TO HOTEL HOUSEKEEPING MANAGEMENT

• Checking bathroom supplies. Replacing the used supplies with the new ones.

• Checking the room curtains and drapes for stains, replacing if needed and closing.

• Discarding the used supplies in the guest room.

• Spraying the room with air freshener.

Cleaning an Occupied Room

If the room is cleaned while the guest is present, proper decorum and respect must be maintained. Although talking with the guest is allowed, it is best to speak when spoken to rather than initiate conversations.

• Enter the guest room by following the set procedure.

• Clear the dustbins.

• Collect the used linen and put it in the linen bag.

• Make the bed.

• Carry out the guest room dusting.

• Vacuum the carpet and bedside mats.

A SIMPLE GUIDE TO HOTEL HOUSEKEEPING MANAGEMENT

- Clean the bathroom and replenish the bathroom supplies.

- Check the functionality of light bulbs, television, electric kettle and intercom device.

Cleaning the Check-Out Room

This cleaning is performed when the guest vacates the guest room and proceeds for hotel check-out formalities. The cleaning involves:

- Assembling bed, chairs, settees and other furniture and placing it appropriately.

- Wiping the guest room floor with wet mop.

- Cleaning the writing tables, assembling and placing stationery appropriately.

- Checking under the beds, chairs, chests, and in the locker, if included, for any articles the guest left behind.

- All personal stuff, documents, articles left in the room (if any) are removed and deposited to Lost and Found desk.

- Cleaning all walls of bathroom with wet wipes and/or sanitizing mixtures.

Lynton Viñas (Frye)

- Cleaning all electric appliances such as microwave, fan, refrigerator and others.

- Keeping heaters/air conditioners at lowest power consuming option.

- Switching off the room light and television.

- Locking the guest room door and cleaning area outside it.

- Depositing the keys at front office desk.

Periodic Cleaning in Hotel

The task of cleaning is very exhausting. It is divided among a number of housekeeping staff depending upon expertise. Some cleaning, such as occupied guest rooms, might be required twice a day in some cases. The check-in and check-out cleanings are a little less frequent.

Furthermore, the cleaning of the air-conditioner and refrigerator should not be neglected.

Spring Cleaning

This type of cleaning is practiced in hotels located in all regions. The name depicts cleaning the hotel in the first few warm days of spring when there is adequate sunlight to reach the corners and the floors of the room.

Spring cleaning is generally performed once a year by moving furniture and cleaning the guest rooms entirely of accumulated dust, stains and broken furniture.

Cleaning Public Areas of Hotel

The general public areas are shared commonly among guests. They include the Front Office, Lobby and Corridors, and since they are what the guests see first, they must be always kept meticulously clean.

The Front Office and Lobby are highly frequented areas that need constant attention. It must be clean at all hours of the day. The housekeeping staff needs to clean desks, fans, ceilings, chairs and computers. The staff also cleans and disinfects the telephone devices, keyboards, flooring, corridors and glass doors at the entrance of the lobby.

A SIMPLE GUIDE TO HOTEL HOUSEKEEPING MANAGEMENT

Cleaning the Dining Area

The restaurant is sometimes leased out and the operators arrange for its cleaning by their own staff. However, many hotels operate their own restaurants, so the housekeeping staff is assigned the task of keeping it clean and well- sanitized. The housekeeping staff must put in good efforts for lighting, chandeliers, cleaning the ceiling, furniture and décor items. It can, but rarely includes, spreading the clean dining linen on the dining tables. Cleaning is generally done when the area is not busy or when it is closed

Cleaning the Lifts (Elevators)

The housekeeping staff cleans lifts preferably early morning to avoid rush times. They stop it at the ground floor; its doors are kept open and it is then cleaned starting from the top and working towards the bottom.

Cleaning the Swimming Pools

This can be conducted by the hotel if it has in-house expertise, or it can be contracted with an agency. Cleaning of the swimming pool involves catching any leaves, purifying the pool water, and cleaning the areas surrounding the pool; including shower and changing rooms.

Cleaning the Hotel Garden

More luxurious hotels keep their private team of gardeners. Watering and trimming the trees and shrubs, fertilizing the plants, raking the fall leaves, and arbo-sculpture (art of shaping trees) is taken care of by this team.

Cleaning the Parking Area

This mostly involves hard sweeping the parking space, removing the cobwebs under the parking shades and putting up appropriate guiding signs.

Hotel Housekeeping Cleaning Equipment

The staff needs to utilize various cleaning equipment while trying to keep the hotel premises to the highest standard of appearance and there are a wide range of cleaning products available in order to facilitate this which makes it possible to do the job more thoroughly and efficiently.

A SIMPLE GUIDE TO HOTEL HOUSEKEEPING MANAGEMENT

Advantages of Cleaning Equipment

The cleaning equipment is advantageous in multiple ways:

•   Equally effective for general as well as tougher cleaning tasks.

•   High cleaning capability.

•   Reduces work fatigue and increases productivity in a variety of ways which make work more efficient; and thereby, reduces the time element used in cleaning.

•   Saves the time of hotel housekeeping staff.

•   With high manoeuvrability, it can reach any corner or height of the room.

•   It is eco-friendly, widely available and easy to operate.

•   It gives protection from injuries occurring while cleaning, when proper instructions are followed.

Classification of Cleaning Equipment

There are broadly categorized as follows:

Manual Cleaning Equipment

A SIMPLE GUIDE TO HOTEL HOUSEKEEPING MANAGEMENT

As the name suggests, they are used in a manual manner by individual cleaners to keep the surfaces clean. Some commonly used manual equipment are:

- Abrasives – They are the sharpening stones or grit papers used to polish metal or wooden surfaces. There are various abrasives depending upon the size of grit and adhesion of grit particles on the paper.

- Brushes – They are handheld flat brushes with bristles to dust the plain surfaces as well as the corners. They come with non-slip handles and stiff scratch-free bristles. They help in removing stubborn dust.

- Housekeeping Trolley – This trolley is large enough to keep all the guest room and guest bathroom supplies in an organized manner

- Dustbins – They are used to collect daily garbage produced in the hotel.

- Dusting Cloths – They are soft cloths used for wiping the surface dust.

A SIMPLE GUIDE TO HOTEL HOUSEKEEPING MANAGEMENT

- Dustpans – They are used to collect dust and garbage by putting it into the dustbin.

- Janitor's trolley – It is a trolley that stores cleaning supplies such as detergents, spray bottles, dustbins, mops, and dusting cloths, all in a compact manner. It can be moved around easily. It fulfills the challenge of modern day housekeeping in hotels.

- Mops – There are various types of mops such as string mops, flat mops, dust mops and synthetic mops. Mops are generally made of flat cotton strings or heavy-duty sponges fixed on the metal frames. The cotton mops have high absorbing ability but need more care, unlike the synthetic mops that offer almost zero absorbing ability and less maintenance.

- Mop Wringer trolley – A mop bucket cart (or mop trolley) is a wheeled bucket that allows its user to wring out a wet mop without getting the hands dirty. The mops are squeezed between two surfaces to remove dirty water from it.

• Scarifying machine – It is used for properly maintaining gardens, golf courts and lawns on the hotel premises. It cuts through the turf and removes moss and dead grass. It helps grow a spongy lawn. Scarifiers have fixed knife blades attached to the rotary cylinder. They cut through the grass by which the offshoots are separated into lots of individual plants. This helps to thicken up the turf and improve its health.

• Spray Bottles – They are used to spray water or chemical solutions on the surface that needs cleaning and to spray water on the delicate flowers or leaves of flower arrangements.

Scarifying Machine

A SIMPLE GUIDE TO HOTEL HOUSEKEEPING MANAGEMENT

Electric Cleaning Equipment

As the name depicts, this equipment requires electrical power to operate. They are operated either on AC power or on a battery. Some important electrical equipment is:

- Box Sweeper – It is electric sweeper that consists of a friction brush. The brush often is fit to revolve vertically or horizontally when the equipment moves on the surface. It can clean floors as well as carpets. The wider it is the better the box sweeper brush.

- Vacuum Cleaner – It is major equipment in hotel housekeeping. It comes with a suction motor fit in a case, a hose and various attachments for delicate as well as tough cleaning requirements.

- Polishing Machine – They are used to add a shine to the floors of most frequented areas of the hotel.

- Scrubber – It is a floor care accessory that comes with a handheld electrically operated scrubber. It is used where just mopping will not suffice. It can scrub stubborn and sticky stains on the floors of cafeterias, restaurants, lobbies and fitness areas where people can take food and beverages.

• Vapour Cleaning Machine – They are used where the chemical odours are undesirable. They are equipped for continuous operation. They heat up quickly and work with a low amount of moisture. They kill the bed bugs and their eggs, thus yielding a completely clean environment.

Scrubbing Machine   Box Sweeper

Polishing Machine

Vapor Cleaning Machine   Vacuum Cleaner

A SIMPLE GUIDE TO HOTEL HOUSEKEEPING MANAGEMENT

Cleaning Agents or Chemicals

Apart from water and regular detergents, the housekeeping staff also uses cleaning chemicals, which are often available in the form of liquids, blocks and powders.

• Water – It is the most commonly used medium for cleaning and rinsing. The housekeeping staff needs to use only soft water because hard water cannot dilute detergents properly. Non-oily and non-greasy stains such as ink stains can be removed using water.

• Vinegar – It is used in removing light stains in the bath.

• Bathroom Cleaners – They come in liquid form for easy cleaning. They clean, de-scale, and disinfect the bathroom walls, bathtubs, bathroom flooring, sinks and showers. They often contain phosphoric acid.

• Clean Air Sprays – They are best for freshening the hotel corridors, washrooms, bathrooms and reception areas. These sprays remove the pungent smell of tobacco, smoke and organic wastes.

• Degreaser – This is mainly used in bars to remove the marks of grease and lipstick that cannot be removed by traditional washing of glasses and cups. Degreaser restores the surface shine and transparency of glasses and bowls.

Abrasive Handle

Carpet Cleaner   Air Spray   Laundry Detergent

Toilet Rim Blocks   Degreaser   Vinegar   Floor Cleaner

Surface Sanitizer

• Floor Cleaners and Sealers – One of the important tasks of hotel housekeeping is cleaning the floor periodically and keeping it sealed with the help of a sealer of the right consistency for optimum maintenance. Some areas in the hotel are busy and bear heavy traffic such as the lobby, corridors, parking areas, restaurants and dining halls. Their floorings lose smoothness and shine. In such a case, the floor cleaners and sealers are used for restoring their look and shine.

• Laundry Cleaners – They are liquid concentrates with variable amounts of peroxide that removes tough stains, bleaches the linen and enhances its whiteness.

A number of chemicals are used in dry-cleaning. They are camphor oil, turpentine spirits, benzene, kerosene and white gasoline, petroleum solvents such as naphtha blends, chloroform, carbon tetrachloride and liquid carbon dioxide. They remove the stains from silk tapestry without damaging the fibres.

• Surface Sanitizers – They often come in the form of liquid concentrate. They are water-based and sanitize the surfaces without damaging their appearance. The sanitizers reduce the presence of bacteria to a great extent. They come with different concentrations and fragrances.

• Toilet Blocks – They deodorize the toilets and leave them with a fresh smell. They come with two variants: continuous action and instant action. They contain oxidizing agents such as ozone, hydrogen peroxide or chlorine that removes unpleasant organic odour from the surface of a material.

• Toilet Cleaners – They are available in liquid form containing strong hydrochloric acid. They remove stains and plumbing scales easily and restore the surface shine.

• Carpet Cleaning Agents – Cleaning and maintaining the carpets are important tasks of hotel housekeeping. As suggested by the Carpet and Rug Institute (CRI), carpet cleaning is complete when the following issues are tackled :

Soil containment

A SIMPLE GUIDE TO HOTEL HOUSEKEEPING MANAGEMENT

Vacuuming

Spotting

Interim cleaning

Restorative cleaning

Carpet cleaning chemicals are often low-moisture, fast-drying cleaners that take care of the above said issues effectively.

• Swimming Pool Cleaners – They are used for cleaning the swimming pool water. The pool cleaning chemicals kill the bacterial and algae growth in the water.

Hotel Housekeeping – In Room Guest Supplies

The housekeeping staff prepares the guest room and the other places in the hotel so that the guest is comfortable; therefore, the housekeeping staff places some necessary supplies in the guest rooms and guest bathrooms.

As per the hotel policy and the standard of the room, the lists of these supplies may change. The housekeeping staff needs to ensure that those supplies are kept in appropriate numbers and condition while preparing a room for guest check-in.

List of Supplies for a Guest Room

The guest room supplies are considered as guest essentials. The housekeeping staff places the following standard supplies in the guest room:

• Furniture – It includes bed, bedside table, chairs, wardrobe with locker facility, writing table, dressing table, center table and usually a magazine holder.

• Bedding – It includes mattress, bed sheet, bed cover, quilt, quilt cover, pillows and cases.

• Bedside Supplies – They include non-slip mats on the either sides of the bed.

• Bedside Table Supplies – They involve a telephone device, and a printed compiled list of important intercom numbers such as reception, restaurant and the laundry of the hotel. The housekeeping staff also provides a copy of the Bible, Geeta or Koran, depending upon the prior knowledge of the guest's religious orientation.

A SIMPLE GUIDE TO HOTEL HOUSEKEEPING MANAGEMENT

- Centre Table Supplies – It includes room service, laundry service and spa and health club rate cards. It also has an ash tray, if smoking is allowed, and a small decorative center piece.

- Clothing and Clothing Care – It involves bathrobe, coffee table cover, rocking chair cover and hangers for clothes and ties.

- Hospitality Tray – It is a small tray with compartments that holds sachets of coffee, tea, cocoa powder, creamer and sugar. Some hotels also offer the sachets of condiments like black and white pepper powder and salt. They also keep an electric kettle, a couple of cups, saucers, spoons, and water bottle so that the guest can make the beverage of his or her choice.

- Mini Bar Supplies – It includes a small personal refrigerator filled with soft drinks, alcoholic drinks, soda and ice cubes. It may also include salted peanuts, cashew nuts or chips.

- Writing Desk Supplies – A writing pad, a pencil, an eraser, promotional brochures, La carte menu and the short list of places of historical and commercial importance in the city for the guest's reference.

List of Supplies for Guest Bathroom

They are also considered as guest essentials. The guests are expected to use these supplies or take them away on departure. Depending upon the type of room, the list of supplies for the guest bathroom are:

• Bathroom Attachments – Bath area with shower and handheld shower attachments, a bath tub with hot-cold water mixer and handheld shower attachment, soap dispenser, toilet paper attachment, towel holder and a basin with hot-cold water mixer attachment.

• Towels – A couple of pairs of large and small towels each for the guests to be used according to their requirement.

• Dustbin – A small dustbin with lid, which can be often opened by the foot and lined with a plastic bag from inside.

A SIMPLE GUIDE TO HOTEL HOUSEKEEPING MANAGEMENT

•   Non-slip Foot-mat – It is often kept near the bathtub.

•   Slippers – Flat non-slip slippers for the guest.

•   Mirror – A large mirror is often fitted on the wall above the basin.

•   Hair Dryer – A wall mounted fixed hair dryer for the guest is kept in the bathrooms.

•   Vanity Tray – It contains small bottles of shower gel, shampoo and conditioner. Some hotels also provide moisturizer, shower cap, hand and foot cream, ear buds and a small manicure kit. It may also contain a couple of empty glasses, disposable toothbrushes and a small bottle of mouthwash.

Bathroom Slippers   Bath Linen   Bath Robe   Floor Mat

Hair Dryer   Vanity Kit

A SIMPLE GUIDE TO HOTEL HOUSEKEEPING MANAGEMENT

Items Provided on Request

The items provided on request are given to the guests when they ask for them. These are the supplies apart from regular supplies required by some guests. These are often provided as guest expendables. Some of them are:

- Alarm clock
- Comb
- Crib or Cradle
- Disposable Diapers
- Disposable razor
- Electric blanket
- Electric fan
- Extra blankets
- First aid medical kit
- Handheld shower attachment
- Hearing equipment
- Hot water bag
- Iron
- Ironing board
- Pillow

A SIMPLE GUIDE TO HOTEL HOUSEKEEPING MANAGEMENT

- Potty Ring for toilet
- Raised toilet seat
- Sanitary napkins
- Sewing kit
- Stationery items
- Tampons
- Wipes

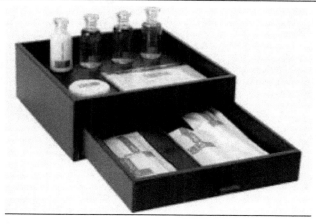

A SIMPLE GUIDE TO HOTEL HOUSEKEEPING MANAGEMENT

Lynton Viñas (Frye)

Chapter 6

Room Area Procedures

Hotel Housekeeping – Standard Procedures

The effort of the housekeeping staff speaks volumes about the hotel's commitment to the guest's comfort. The results of sincere, as well as faux housekeeping efforts, are highly noticeable. The housekeeping staff needs to execute cleaning and maintenance tasks at various places inside the hotel. The most important task is cleaning and maintaining guest rooms and guest bathrooms.

A SIMPLE GUIDE TO HOTEL HOUSEKEEPING MANAGEMENT

The guests expectation of cleanliness in these two areas is critical to a hotel's success.

By following the absolute best cleaning and maintenance practices, the housekeeping staff can contribute to retaining the loyalty of satisfied guests as well as generating new guests willing to visit the hotel. This generates more revenue for the hotel as a result of a positive image. To elevate guest satisfaction and work productively together, the housekeeping staff needs to structure the cleaning and maintenance procedures and follow them appropriately.

Setting the Chambermaid's Trolley

The chambermaid's trolley can be viewed as a large tool box on wheels to aid the hotel housekeeping staff. It has a number of compartments and shelves of various sizes. This trolley is filled with the materials from the housekeeping supplies store at the end of each shift, so that the next shift staff can access it immediately.

Lynton Viñas (Frye)

A SIMPLE GUIDE TO HOTEL HOUSEKEEPING MANAGEMENT

The staff considers the following points while loading the chambermaid's trolley.

•   Loading the trolley with adequate supplies, depending upon the number and types of the rooms on the floor.

•   Avoiding overloading the trolley that may lead to accidents.

•   Avoiding under-loading the trolley which may lead to making unnecessary trips to the supplies store.

SOP for Setting the Chambermaid's Trolley

•   Empty the trolley.

- Check repeatedly for any broken parts.

- Clean it by dusting and wiping any stains.

- Place the items according to their weight: heaviest items at the bottom and lighter items at the top section of the trolley.

- Place the linen for different purposes separately.

- Close the lids of cleaner bottles and liquid cans tightly.

- Record the numbers and types of the items loaded in the trolley.

- Collect the room keys.

- Take the trolley to the assigned duty floor.

- Park it outside the room in a manner that the linen side faces outside and the room entrance is blocked.

SOP for Entering the Guest Room

The housekeeping staff should follow the SOP given below for entering the guest room.

- Leave the DND (Do not Disturb) rooms undisturbed.

A SIMPLE GUIDE TO HOTEL HOUSEKEEPING MANAGEMENT

• Knock on the door with knuckles and announce in pleasant voice, "Housekeeping."

• Wait for five seconds to hear the response.

• In case of no response, announce the same again.

• In there is no answer second time, open the door with the key.

• Enter the room.

• If the guest is found sleeping, withdraw from the room quietly.

• In case the guest answers, ask politely when would he or she want service.

• In case the guest wants it later, acknowledge his or her reply and withdraw from the room.

• If the housekeeping work is in progress and the guest returns, greet him or her and ask if it is alright for you to continue cleaning.

SOPs for Cleaning the Guest Room

Once the staff enters the room and starts the housekeeping work, he or she must:

A SIMPLE GUIDE TO HOTEL HOUSEKEEPING MANAGEMENT

- Not use guest room linen as a door stopper or for cleaning and dusting the room.

- Keep the guest room door open while working.

- Open the curtains and patio door.

- Assemble the furniture and place appropriately.

- Keep the vacuum cleaner and other cleaning apparatus in the room.

- Take the bed linen of appropriate size and place it on the nearest chair.

- Remove previous bedspread and place on the chair.

- Inspect the bed and pillows for their condition as well as for any lost-and-found.

- In case of checkout room, deposit the left guest items with the floor supervisor. If the room is still occupied by the guest, place the item so that it is safe as well as visible to the guest.

- Put soiled sheets and pillow covers in the soiled linen cart of the trolley.

Lynton Viñas (Frye)

A SIMPLE GUIDE TO HOTEL HOUSEKEEPING MANAGEMENT

•   Empty ashtrays and rubbish from the guest room and bathroom dustbins into the trash cart on the trolley.

•   Pick up used glasses, mugs, ashtrays, trays, and place them on the bathroom platform.

•   Spray the bathtub, basin, glasses, mugs, and trays with cleaning liquid. Let them soak in the chemicals from the liquid.

•   Make the bed.

•   Start dusting from an extreme inside corner of the room and work outwards.

•   Clean wipe TV.

•   Straighten the guest items.

•   Sweep the room and patio floor.

•   Mop the room and patio floor.

•   Clean the glasses, mugs and trays.

•   Sanitize glasses, mugs, the telephone device and TV remote.

•   Inspect the condition of bathroom slippers and bathrobe. Replace if soiled.

•   Close the patio door.

- Close all the curtains.

- Clean the entrance door.

- Close and lock the room door.

- Report any damage spotted to the supervisor.

SOPs for Cleaning the Guest Bathroom

The SOP for cleaning the guest bathroom is given below.

- Open bathroom ventilation.

- Sweep the bathroom floor.

- Scrub and finish the platform, bathtub and basin.

- Scrub and finish the toilet bowl, rim, ring and hinge.

- Wipe the mirror.

- Clean bathroom walls using wet mop or sponge.

- Replace the bathroom amenities such as toilet roll, toilet block, shampoo, conditioners and moisturizers.

- Replace bathroom mat.

- Wipe down shower curtain working from top to bottom with a dry cloth.

- Replace bath towels and hand towels.

- Replace the dustbin liner.

- Close the bathroom ventilation.

- Clean the bathroom door.

- Keep the bathroom door open after cleaning.

- Check bathroom doormat. Replace if required.

- Report any damage spotted to the supervisor.

SOPs for Cleaning Balcony / Patio

The balcony or the patios are the extensions of the guest room. The SOPs for cleaning them are given below.

- Enter the balcony.

- Spray walls, railings

- Scrub and clean the bird droppings

- Wipe down rocking or sitting chairs and table

- Clean the door tracks appearing on the floor.

- Sweep the floor.

- Mop the floor.

SOPs for Do-Not-Disturb (DND) Rooms

Every room has to be entered at least once a day by the housekeeping staff. The guests who do not want to get disturbed by any housekeeping service tag their rooms with a Do-Not-Disturb (DND) sign.

The SOP for these rooms are given below.

- Do not disturb by placing a call until 2:00 o'clock in the afternoon.

- After 2:00 p.m., the Supervisor calls the room to know the guest's needs.

- The housekeeping staff contacts the supervisor to make sure whether or not to service the room.

- If the call made to the room is not answered by the guest after two calling attempts, the room is serviced.

- To the best judgement, the housekeeping staff enters the room and continues with the usual housekeeping work.

Public Area Cleaning SOP

There are various public areas in the hotel frequented by the guests. The areas and their respective SOPs for housekeeping are as given below:

SOPs for Cleaning the Lifts

- Carry out the lift cleaning task early morning when the least number of guests are expected to use it.

- Call the elevator on the ground floor.

- Open its door.

- Put appropriate signboard near it.

- Clean the lift using the appropriate cleaning liquid according to the wall material of the lift cabin.

- Wipe the lift doors.

- Work from top to bottom while cleaning a lift cabin.

• Keep the lift door open until the floor and walls are dried completely.

• Spray clean air freshener all about to mask any odours.

SOPs for Cleaning the Front Office and Lobby

The lobby is active 24 hours. The furniture, carpets, flooring and ceiling; everything needs to be kept extremely clean at any given time. The SOPs are as follows:

• For any areas that allow smoking, clear all ashtrays into the trash ensuring no cigarettes are burning.

• Clean and restore them to proper places.

• Clear the dustbins near front office desk.

• Replace their lining and keep them as they were.

• Dust and wipe the telephone device, fax machine, computers and kiosks. Sanitize the telephone device, computer key board and touchpad of the kiosk.

• Remove spider webs from ceiling.

A SIMPLE GUIDE TO HOTEL HOUSEKEEPING MANAGEMENT

• Remove the dust deposited on walls, windows, furniture and floor.

• Remove stains on the carpet and furniture.

• Clean all artefacts using damp and soft cloth carefully.

• Sweep and mop the flooring of lobby and front office desk area.

• Dust and polish any vases, paintings and art pieces.

• Spray with fresh air clean spray with signature aroma.

• Play a very light and soothing instrumental music.

SOPs for Cleaning Parking Area

The parking area takes the load of pollution created by hotel owned vehicles and guests' private vehicles. It is heavily polluted with dirt and dust. The parking area needs cleanliness with respect to the following terms:

• Control the ventilation.

A SIMPLE GUIDE TO HOTEL HOUSEKEEPING MANAGEMENT

- Control pollutant discharges occurring from broken drainage or water systems of the hotel.

- Remove fine-grained sediment particles on parking floor.

- Clean the area near lift.

- Hard-sweep the parking floor using street sweeping equipment.

- Collect and dispose all the debris appropriately.

- Bring the presence of any unusual debris to the notice of public area supervisor.

SOPs for Keeping the Garden

Some places, the housekeeping staff works to keep the garden looking beautiful. They must:

- Water the plants regularly according to the season and requirement of the plants; generally early morning.

- Remove the weed and fall leaves daily.

- Implement Arbosculpture to enhance the beauty of the trees and bushes.

Lynton Viñas (Frye)

- Keep the gardening tools clean and safe.

- Report any damage or requirement of tools or plants to the public area supervisor.

- Keep the lawn grass in healthy condition by periodic cutting with the help of scarifying machine.

- Keep any artificial waterfalls or artificial water body clean.

- Fertilizing plants as per the schedule.

- Recycle the food wastage in the hotel to prepare organic fertilizer.

SOPs for Cleaning the Dining Area

The dining areas need daily cleaning before the restaurant working hours start as well as when the restaurant staff requests cleaning. The SOP is given below.

- Collect all the cleaning equipment and dining area keys.

- Switch on all the electric lamps.

- Open all the drapes and blinds for letting in the natural light.

A SIMPLE GUIDE TO HOTEL HOUSEKEEPING MANAGEMENT

- Observe the entire area to plan the work.

- Align all the chairs away from the table to make room for cleaning.

- Clean the carpet area, using vacuum cleaner.

- Remove any food stains from the carpet using appropriate cleaner.

- If there is no carpet on the floor, sweep and mop it.

- Dust all the furniture in the dining area.

- Polish the furniture, if required.

- Using a feather duster, dust all the pictures, paintings, artworks and corners.

- Clean and disinfect the telephone devices.

- Polish metal, glass, and wood items.

- Clean the mirrors and windows by wiping them with a wet sponge.

- If a requirement for maintenance is spotted, consult the engineering department.

- If any guest items are found, then deposit them with the housekeeping control desk.

Lynton Viñas (Frye)

- Collect all dirty table linens and replace with fresh ones.

- Return the keys to the security department.

- Record in the housekeeping register.

SOPs for Cleaning the Swimming Pool

The swimming pool cleaning activity can be conducted in-house by training and employing special housekeeping staff. There could be separate swimming pools such as indoor and outdoor as well as for adults and for children. The following steps are taken to clean and maintain the swimming pool, assuming that is a task assigned to housekeeping:

- Check water quality more than once a week.

- Check any broken tiles/pipes inside the swimming pool.

- Clean the water as soon as possible when required.

- Check the pool water for contamination daily. Remove leaves using leaf catchers.

• Check for slippery floor area and the pool bottom. Apply and maintain the anti-slip mats near the pool. Scrub and clean the bottom of the pool.

• Keep the life-saving and floating apparatus ready all time.

• Keep poolside area and basking chairs clean.

• Keep appropriate and highly noticeable signages showing the depth of the swimming pool.

• Check and keep changing rooms up to the highest quality.

• Keep the changing room door open when it is not occupied.

• If using employee lifeguards, provide general safety check for swimming pool once a day during the operating hours.

• Add adequate amount of chlorine in the pool water.

Chapter 7

Procedural Issues

Certain types of cleaning are not done on a continuous basis due to time constraints and financial considerations, but many can be done periodically in order to elevate the level of cleanliness.

<u>SOPs for Spring Cleaning</u>

Since Spring-cleaning is a time intensive process and it is conducted during a low occupancy period. The standard procedures are:

A SIMPLE GUIDE TO HOTEL HOUSEKEEPING MANAGEMENT

- Request a spring-cleaning date from the front office desk. (The housekeeping department needs to honour whatever date they give, as it is the matter of revenue generation.)

- Tag the room as "Not for Use."

- Remove the guest amenities, curtains, and art pieces from the room.

- Send the curtains to the laundry for dry cleaning.

- Empty the mini bar and send the beverage items to Food and Beverage store.

- Roll the curtains and cover them with dustsheet.

- Inspect the furniture and send any items needing repair out or have someone come in to repair the furniture and upholstery.

- Inspect all the locks, knobs, latches and for leaking pipes.

- Hand over the room to maintenance department for any painting, sealing and repairing work that might be required.

Lynton Viñas (Frye)

A SIMPLE GUIDE TO HOTEL HOUSEKEEPING MANAGEMENT

• Once the maintenance work is complete, remove any residual smell of paint and varnish by airing the room.

• Polish and clean the permanent fixtures.

• Open, lay and shampoo any carpets.

• Check the bathroom ceiling and clean the bathroom.

• Make the bed using fresh bed linen.

• Restore the art pieces, furniture and guest supplies.

• Call room service for restocking mini bar, glasses and trays.

• Show the room to the floor supervisor.

• Release it to the front office desk for letting.

SOPs for Closing Down the Shifts

The floor supervisor closes the shift formally by ensuring the following points from the cleaning attendants

• Empty garbage bags of the chambermaid's trolley into the garbage receptacle.

A SIMPLE GUIDE TO HOTEL
HOUSEKEEPING MANAGEMENT

- Ensure the soiled linen is collected into chambermaid's trolley bags are sent to laundry.

- Remove the chambermaid's trolley and check it for any damage and dirt accumulation.

- Empty the vacuum cleaner bags and replace them with new ones.

- Tidy the housekeeping department area by stacking the items at their appropriate places.

- Clean the toilet brushes with hot water for ten minutes every week.

- Rinse mops in light detergents and hang for drying.

- Close the doors and hand over the keys to the housekeeping control desk.

- Sign off the shift.

Hotel Housekeeping – Linen Maintenance

In the range of small to large hotels, the guest room linen, guest bathroom linen and staff uniforms accumulate in large amounts. It is essential for the housekeeping staff to launder the linen and make it readily available at all times so that the staff can receive their well-laundered uniforms before work and the guests are provided with good quality linen. (Sometimes this process is outsourced.)

Purchasing good quality linen is an absolute must; but the life, appearance and the quality of linen largely depends upon the treatment it receives at the laundry by the laundry staff. Small hotels can contract with commercial laundry services located outside the hotel. Large hotel establishments prefer to install their private on-premises laundry. Let us review on-premises laundries operated by housekeeping.

Advantages of On-Premise Laundry

The following advantages are apparent if the housekeeping staff uses on-premise laundry:

• On-premise laundry provides more use with comparatively less investment.

• The time, energy and effort to take the clothes outside at a commercial laundry service is eliminated; hence, the staff can work better.

• The housekeeping staff can easily access the on-premise laundry.

• Pilferage is reduced.

• The staff can have complete control over the wash cycles and the wear and tear of the linen. Thus, life of the fabric can be prolonged.

On-Premise Laundry Equipment

On-premise laundry is effective in the conservation of water and electricity and the generation of high through-put. This equipment speeds up the housekeeping work. The laundry equipment may include:

1. Washer/Extractors

They are automatic machines which are used to wash the linen in large amounts. They provide high laundry room productivity by using less water and electricity.

2. Dryers

They dry the linen in less time than conventional drying methods. They deliver fast drying without consuming much electrical energy.

A SIMPLE GUIDE TO HOTEL
HOUSEKEEPING MANAGEMENT

Washers

Dryers

Ironer

Folder

3. Flatwork Ironers

They save energy, cost and effort to press the large number of linens by delivering them ironed and pressed. They are easy and safe to operate.

4. Commercial Folders and Stackers

They are additional automatic laundry devices that can deliver a perfectly folded and finished linen. They can also help to stack the folded linen neatly. The housekeeping staff that handles laundry is expected to know each device and understand its operation.

Working at On-Premise Hotel Laundry

The laundry consists of all bath and bed linens, dining area linens, staff uniforms, cleaning cloths, curtains, drapes, blankets, ancillary cloth items and rugs. The guest laundry is handled by the most experienced staff. The staff in the laundry room is expected to be aware of the chemicals, detergents, dry cleaning agents and the stages of the laundry cycle.

No sooner than the soiled laundry arrives, the laundering work should begin. The reasons behind this are:

- The soiled linen must be cleaned as early as possible.

- The stains may get permanent.

- The stains may get transferred to other linen.

- The soiled linen should not provide a breeding ground for bacteria.

- To avoid the chances of linen being misplaced or lost.

Laundry Cycle

The laundry goes through the following stages:

SOPs for Laundry Management

Laundry management is carried out on daily basis. Here are some standard procedures:

- Collect Dirty Linen – Collect the dirty linen from various sections in the hotel such as guest rooms, guest bathrooms and the dining area. Put the soiled linen separately. The principle is, whatever linen it is, it must not hang over the edge of the collection basket. Transfer the collected linen to the laundry department.

A SIMPLE GUIDE TO HOTEL HOUSEKEEPING MANAGEMENT

• Sort the Linen – Segregate the linen carefully according to type of fabric, domain of item use, degree of soiling and type of soiling. Keep the staff uniforms, guest room and bathroom linen, dining area linen, butchery aprons and guests' personal clothes all separate. Always handle the linen using gloves.

• Pre-treat the Stains – Before putting the linen into the washing machine, inspect it for stains such as grease or oil. Remove the stains using stain cleaning chemicals. If instructed beforehand, use detergents and cleaning chemicals at the time of washing only to save the time and effort.

• Wash/Extract the Linen – Put the linen into washers. Weigh the linen before washing process to ensure the washers are not overloaded. The housekeeping staff needs to handle many washers and dryers depending on the size of hotel and occupancy of the rooms. Set the automatic washers to different wash cycles depending upon the type of linen. For example, embroidered pillow covers need soft wash cycle and the curtains need harder wash cycles.

The following wash cycle is most effective:

Soak → Flush → Suds → Bleach → Rinse → Extract → Starch

• Remove as much as possible water content from the linen by using extractors. The linens are then starched to make it look stiff and shiny.

• Dry the Linen − Put the linen into dryers for removing any moisture still left. Be careful while transferring the linen from washers to dryers because the weight of the linen increases after washing. Use automatic dryer that provides drying by hot air blows. The lint comes off from the linen surface in the process of drying yielding a finished surface. These dryers operate on less electricity and yield fresh and completely dry linen.

• Iron/Repair the Linen − At this stage, check the linen for any wear and tear. Separate the worn out linen to be given to the tailor. Some linen such as towels, bed linen and dining area linen require Ironing. Pass these linen through the ironer. Hand-iron some linen, such as uniforms.

• Fold and Stack the Linen − Automatic folding and stacking machines come to the aid of housekeeping staff to save them from the effort of folding and stacking the linen accurately. Some types of linen, such as staff uniforms and guest personal clothes still need manual efforts for folding. Operate the folding/stacking machine that ascertains finished appearance and makes the linen easy for storage and handling.

• Deliver the Linen − Transport the ready laundered linen to the uniform room and linen room. Send the linen that needs repair to the tailor room. Then, subsequently deliver all the linen at the appropriate time for cleaning the various premises such as guest rooms, the dining areas and banquet halls.

Chapter 8

Coordination

Success is not created by one person, but by a dedicated team. ....Lynton Viñas Frye

If various departments are seen as organs of the body, then the housekeeping department can be seen as a mesh of nerves that coordinates with various organs to achieve its objectives.

No work in the industry is complete without precise coordination and detailed documentation. The housekeeping department is not an exception either. It needs to coordinate within the department itself and with other departments in the hotel.

Importance of Housekeeping Control Desk

The housekeeping control desk is the hub or a single point of contact for all hotel housekeeping staff. At the control desk, information is fetched, and it is distributed among the relevant staff.

As the housekeeping work is mainly oriented towards providing the best service to the guests, this department needs to work towards sharing information without any communication gaps.

This desk personnel also needs to ensure that the coordination among the housekeeping staff and all other departments of the hotel goes runs in a highly smooth way.

Functions of Housekeeping Control Desk

The hotel control desk performs the following functions:

- Collecting all requests made by the guests.

- Briefing the staff about the routine or special events preparation before the staff begings its routines.

- Assigning routine duties / changed duties to the housekeeping staff.

- Collecting work reports from staff.

- Collecting check-out room numbers and updating it to the floor supervisor.

- Handling the key cabinet that contains the all floors' master keys and housekeeping store keys.

- Maintaining various records on forms and registers.

A SIMPLE GUIDE TO HOTEL HOUSEKEEPING MANAGEMENT

Coordination of Housekeeping with Other Departments

The housekeeping department needs to coordinate with the following departments:

Housekeeping-Front Office Coordination

• Sharing occupancy information that helps to estimate future occupancy, budget and required number of staff.

• Cleaning public areas of hotel premises.

• Special attention requirements like VIP guests, corporate or large family groups or airline crews as occupants.

• Collection of soiled uniforms from and provision of ready uniforms to the front-office staff daily.

Housekeeping-Food and Beverage Coordination

• Forthcoming banquet events and parties.

• Pest control in kitchen and other areas.

• Collection of soiled linen and uniforms from the F&B Department and provision of ready linen and uniforms to the F&B staff daily.

Lynton Viñas (Frye)

A SIMPLE GUIDE TO HOTEL HOUSEKEEPING MANAGEMENT

- Clearance of trays from guest corridors.

- Placement of special guest amenities in guest rooms such as VIP amenities or welcome drink.

Housekeeping-Sales and Marketing Department Coordination

- Supply of promotional brochures, rate cards or other items such as pen stand in the guest rooms.

- Collection of soiled uniforms from the S&M department and provision of ready uniforms to the S&M staff daily.

Housekeeping and the Human Resources Department Coordination

- Acquisition of new staff for the housekeeping department.

- Compensation of housekeeping staff members such as salary, over time, medical treatment, etc.

- Motivation for staff performance through appraisal, induction and training

- Collection of soiled uniforms from the HRD and provision of ready uniforms to the HRD staff daily.

Housekeeping-Security Department Coordination

- Safety of hotel property and keys.

- Prevention of fire and thefts in the hotel.

- Prevention of any suspicious activities, gambling or smuggling performed by guests in the guest rooms or the hotel premises.

- Collection of soiled uniforms from the HRD and provision of ready uniforms to the HRD staff daily.

Housekeeping-Uniformed Service Department Coordination

- Collection of soiled uniforms from the porters, doormen, drivers and provision of ready uniforms to them daily.

Housekeeping-Accounts Department Coordination

It takes place regarding:

- The issues related to payments of housekeeping staff.

• Collection of soiled uniforms from the Accounts Department and provision of ready uniforms to the accounts staff.

Housekeeping-Engineering Department

• The issues related to erroneous functioning of cleaning and gardening equipment, faulty electric power points, leaking pipes, air-conditioning maintenance or any other such work.

• Collection of soiled uniforms from the Engineering and Technology staff and provision of ready uniforms to them daily.

Housekeeping-Maintenance Department

• The repairing and maintenance of broken furniture and fixtures.

• The painting of the required areas in the hotel.

• Repairing pipes and electric points in the guest rooms.

• Collection of soiled uniforms from the Maintenance staff and provision of ready uniforms to them daily.

A SIMPLE GUIDE TO HOTEL HOUSEKEEPING MANAGEMENT

<u>Important Registers Maintained by Housekeeping</u>

The registers are used to record important information. They are very helpful when the shifts and staff on duty changes and while working. The registers serve the purpose of keeping clear and timely records; thereby, fostering accurate communication. Here are some important registers maintained by the housekeeping control desk:

Departure Register

It is kept to track the changes of guest room status such as V, VD, or VC after the guest has checked out. It also tracks the amount of mini bar beverages consumption in the CO guest rooms.

Expected Arrival Register

It keeps the track of pre-registered guests and their profile as Regular/VIP/Other, Marital status, expected check-in time and any special requests to be fulfilled.

Room Status Register

This register records the list of all rooms and their current status.

A SIMPLE GUIDE TO HOTEL HOUSEKEEPING MANAGEMENT

Guest Call Register

It records the instructions or notes relevant to the guest rooms and adjacent area. It is very useful in keeping the track of activities and their durations.

Guest Loan Register

This register is constantly maintained to record the delivery and recovery of the lent items given to the guests. The general format of this register is as follows:

Missing Article Register

If any article owned by the hotel (other than normal consumable items) is found missing in a Check-Out room, then it is recorded in this Register.

Guest Supplies Control Register

This register is maintained to record guest supplies. The general format is as shown below.

Damage/Breakage Register

If any hotel property placed in the guest room is found damaged or broken, it is recorded in this Register.

A SIMPLE GUIDE TO HOTEL HOUSEKEEPING MANAGEMENT

Lost/Found Register

If a housekeeping guest room attendant finds any guest-owned article left in the Check-Out room then it is recorded into the Lost/Found Register and sent to the same cell of the housekeeping department. It also records any personal article found on the hotel premises.

Key Register

It is a register for noting the issued keys of the guest rooms, mater keys of the rooms and important safes and floor keys.

Linen Control Register

This register records the movement of linen between the hotel or outsourced laundry and the guest rooms or dining area. It makes it easy for the housekeeping staff to keep the track of cleaned and soiled laundry.

Checklists and Reports in Housekeeping

There are various housekeeping checklists and reports automatically generated by the hotel management software.

Lynton Viñas (Frye)

A SIMPLE GUIDE TO HOTEL HOUSEKEEPING MANAGEMENT

Checklists

Checklists help to ensure all work is done appropriately without anything left to be completed. There are various checklists filled-in by the housekeeping staff. Some important ones are:

- Guest Supplies Checklist
- Guest Room Cleaning Checklist
- Guest Bathroom Cleaning Checklist
- Beach Area Cleaning Checklist
- Swimming Pool Cleaning Checklist
- Garden Keeping Checklist
- Housekeeping Standard Checklist for Spa
- Housekeeping Standard Checklist for Fitness Centre

Reports

The reports are useful to study past records of occupancy, cleaning schedules and predict the future status of the individual rooms. Let us review some of the reports generated for the hotel Housekeeping Department.

A SIMPLE GUIDE TO HOTEL HOUSEKEEPING MANAGEMENT

Housekeeping Report

This can be generated at the end of each shift to report the housekeeping status of each room.

Housekeeping Assignment Report

It is required for scheduling the room attendants and recording the room inspections.

Housekeeping Occupancy Report

This report shows the list of guests who have checked-in the hotel with details such as number of adults and children, number of nights and housekeeping status. This report is generated for the occupied rooms, rooms expected to be occupied, checked-out rooms, vacant or blocked rooms and details the scheduling of rooms for cleaning.

A SIMPLE GUIDE TO HOTEL HOUSEKEEPING MANAGEMENT

Don't miss these

exciting hospitality books

by Lynton Viñas (Frye)

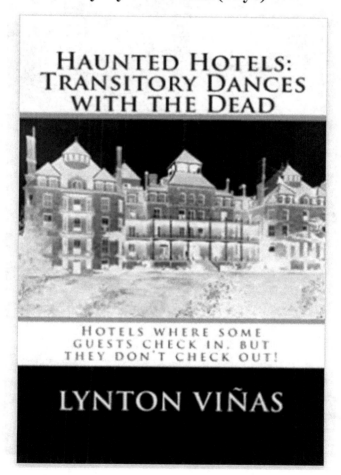

124   **Lynton Viñas (Frye)**

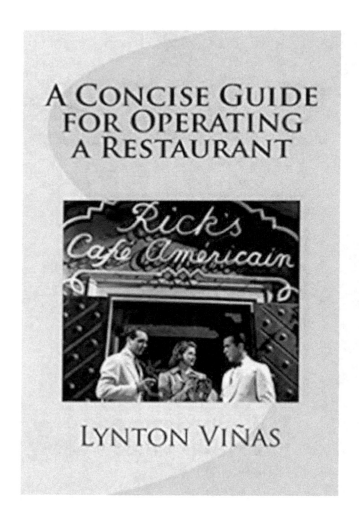